BRAZIL

BRIAN DICKS

☑®

Facts On File, Inc.

Brazil

Facts On File, Inc.
132 West 31st Street
New York NY 10001

Library of Congress Cataloging-in-Publication-Data is on file with the publisher.

Facts On File books are available at special discounts when purchased in bulk quantities for businesses, associations, institutions, or sales promotions. Please call our Special Sales Department in New York at (212) 967-8800 or (800) 322-8755.

You can find Facts On File on the World Wide Web at http://www.factsonfile.com

Printed in China by Imago

10 9 8 7 6 5 4 3 2 1

Editor: Polly Goodman
Designer: Jane Hawkins
Map artwork: Peter Bull
Charts and graphs: Encompass Graphics, Ltd.
Photographs: all by Edward Parker except imprint and contents pages, 17,
                     61 (Corbis Digital Stock); 39 (STR/Reuters, Popperfoto)

Endpapers (front): São Paulo, Brazilís largest city and the third-largest city in the world.
Title page: The town of Olinda and, in the background, Recife.
Imprint and Contents page: The Iguaçu Falls, one of the natural wonders of the world.
Endpapers (back): A fishing trip in Amazonia.

First published by Evans Brothers Limited, 2A Portman Mansions, Chiltern Street, London W1U 6NR, United Kingdom.

CONTENTS

The Brazilian flag. The green and yellow colors stand for forests and minerals. The blue sphere bears the motto *Ordem e progressso* meaning "Order and Progress." The 27 stars, arranged in the pattern of the night sky over Rio de Janeiro, represent Brazil's states and federal district.

INTRODUCING BRAZIL

Large areas of Brazil are wilderness: rugged, forested, isolated and little explored.

B razil is the world's fifth-largest country in both area and population. It is also the largest country in South America, covering some 47 percent of the continent's area with over 51 percent of its population. Only Russia, Canada, China and the United States (including Alaska and Hawaii) are greater in area. Brazil shares borders with all South American countries except Chile and Ecuador.

At its widest point, the distance from west to east across Brazil is over 5,000km, greater than the distance between New York and Los Angeles. Even greater is the distance from its most northern to its most southern points, between the Guyana border in the north and the south-west border with Uruguay, which is roughly 6,000km. Brazil is so big there are three different time zones across the country, varying three to five hours behind GMT. It is little wonder, therefore, that Brazilians say they live in a "continent" rather than a "country."

A COUNTRY OF EXCESSES

With its huge land size and population, Brazil is a country of excesses. It has the world's largest rain forest and the mightiest river

KEY DATA

Area:	8,547,404km²
Highest Point:	Pico da Neblina (3,014m)
Population:	170.1million (2000)
GDP per Capita:	US$7,037*
Currency:	Real
Capital City:	Brasília

Major Cities: (population 1999)

São Paulo	(16.6 million)
Rio de Janeiro	(10.3 million)
Belo Horizonte	(4.6 million)
Salvador	(3.1 million)
Fortaleza	(2.3 million)
Language:	Portuguese

* Calculated on Purchasing Power Parity basis
Sources: UN Population Division; World Bank; *Der Fischer Weltalmanach 2001, Frankfurt am Main*

system. Its mountains and plateau areas contain some of the world's biggest reserves of industrial and precious minerals, and the country has the world's largest hydroelectric power (HEP) station. It exports more coffee and sugar than any other country. Brazil's Atlantic coast stretches some 7,400km, the longest continuous coastline of any country. It has the world's largest soccer stadiums, the most exotic street carnivals and some of the biggest cities. With its size and resources, Brazil is the giant of South America.

A DIVERSE COUNTRY

Brazil is a diverse country in both landscapes and people. Its population is one of the most varied in the world, a mixture of many cultures from all the continents. Its economy is developing fast, the fastest of South America, and Brazil is now the 49th-richest country in the world. Yet many Brazilians live in extreme poverty and there is a great gap between rich and poor. Despite being the wealthiest South American country, Brazil has an enormous foreign debt, has experienced

Brazil has the fifth-largest population in the world, with over two-thirds of its people under the age of 30 years.

periods of crippling inflation and has major problems of social and economic inequality, illiteracy, pollution and crime.

Yet despite the great gulf between extreme wealth and grinding poverty, in both the cities and the countryside, Brazilians are extremely proud of their country, which manages to function as one nation, drawn together by language and culture. At carnival and soccer games, all Brazilians are equal!

São Paulo is Brazil's largest city and the third-largest city in the world.

CASE STUDY
PORTUGUESE COLONIZATION

During the "Great Age of Discovery," in the late fifteenth century, Spain and Portugal wanted to extend their empires into the Americas. In 1494, the Treaty of Tordesillas divided South America between Portugal and Spain. But the pattern of exploration led to Portugal gaining much more land than the treaty specified. Among the earliest Portuguese sea captains was Pedro Alvares Cabral, who investigated the coasts around Rio de Janeiro (see page 44). Further discoveries followed so that by the end of the sixteenth century almost half of South America had been claimed as a Portuguese colony. It was ruled by a governor-general from Salvador, Brazil's first capital. In 1889, Brazil severed its political links with Portugal and declared itself a republic.

Much of the Amazon basin is flooded in the wet season, from January to June each year.

STATES AND REGIONS

Brazil's official name is *República Federativa do Brasil* (Federal Republic of Brazil). Its capital is Brasília. The huge country is divided into 26 states and a federal district. The federal district is Brasília, the newly planned city that succeeded Rio de Janeiro as Brazil's capital on 21 April 1960.

Each state has its own capital city, governor and parliament. The states are largely self-governing, except where issues of national concern are involved, such as defense, currency and foreign relations. They are controlled by the federal government, headed by an elected president. Between 1964 and 1985, five Brazilian presidents were military leaders who resorted to dictatorship rather than democracy. A new constitution came into force in 1988, with a return to democracy in 1990.

THE REGIONS

As well as its states, Brazil is divided into five large regions. Formed out of groups of states, the regional boundaries are used for administrative and statistical purposes and to help the country's general strategic planning. The regions vary in area and population and have different landscapes, histories and modern issues.

THE NORTH

Most of this region lies within the Amazon basin and is covered by tropical rain forest. Its main issue is environmental protection from uncontrolled economic development.

THE NORTHEAST

The Northeast was Brazil's first area of colonial settlement and it has the most colorful mix of cultures, including strong African influences. The area has crippling poverty and unemployment.

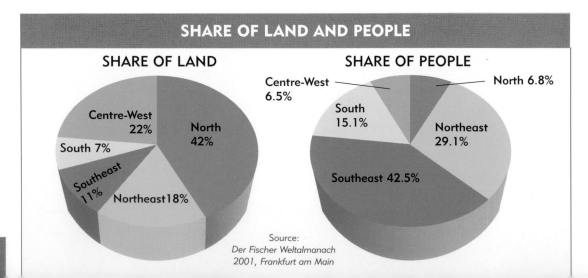

SHARE OF LAND AND PEOPLE

SHARE OF LAND

Centre-West 22%
South 7%
Southeast 11%
Northeast 18%
North 42%

SHARE OF PEOPLE

Centre-West 6.5%
North 6.8%
South 15.1%
Northeast 29.1%
Southeast 42.5%

Source:
Der Fischer Weltalmanach 2001, Frankfurt am Main

THE SOUTHEAST

This is Brazil's economic powerhouse and home to almost half its population. The region's wealth attracts migrants to its large cities, especially São Paulo, Rio de Janeiro and Belo Horizonte.

THE SOUTH

The South is another highly developed region with a more temperate climate than the North. It has attracted immigrants from Germany, Italy and other European countries, whose descendants have kept their languages and customs alive.

THE CENTRE-WEST

Until the 1940s, this region was one of the last great unexplored areas on earth. Although home to the country's capital Brasília, the Centre-West remains largely undeveloped.

Santos is Brazil's major port, in the prosperous Southeast region.

N

COLOMBIA
VENEZUELA
GUYANA
SURINAM
FRENCH GUIANA

Boa Vista
RORAIMA
AMAPÁ
Macapá
Belém
São Luis
Fortaleza

NORTH

Manaus
Trans-Amazonia Highway

AMAZONAS
PARÁ
MARANHÃO
Teresina
CEAR
RIO GRANDE DO NORTE
Natal
João Pessoa
NORTHEAST
PARAÍBA
Recife
PIAUÍ
PERNAMBUCO
ALAGOAS
Maceió

ACRE
Rio Branco
Pôrto Velho
MATO GROSSO
Palmas
TOCANTINS
BAHIA
Aracaju
SERGIPE

PERU
RONDÔNIA
CENTRE-WEST
Salvador

BOLIVIA

Cuiabá
Brasília
MINAS GERAIS
Goiánia
MATO GROSSO DO SUL
GOIÁS
SOUTHEAST
ESPÍRITO SANTO
Belo Horizonte
Vitória
Campo Grande
SÃO PAULO
RIO DE JANEIRO
Rio de Janeiro

PARAGUAY
PARANÁ
São Paulo
SOUTH
Curitiba
SANTA CATARINA
ARGENTINA
RIO GRANDE DO SUL
Florianópolis
Pôrto Alegre

URUGUAY

----- State boundary
▬▬▬ Regional boundary
—— Major roads
········ Main railways
✈ International airports

0   500   1000km
0   600 miles

POPULATION

In northern Brazil, people live in scattered groups throughout the Amazon rain forest.

Only China, India, the United States and Indonesia have larger populations than Brazil. In 2000, the population was 170.1 million, which gave an average population density of just 202 Brazilians living in every square kilometer. But there are great differences in the population density around the country.

POPULATION DISTRIBUTION

Large areas of Brazil have very few people, and some have no people at all. These sparsely populated areas contrast with the immensely overcrowded cities, especially in the Southeast, where official figures are under-estimates and densities can only be guessed. These variations in population distribution are the result of factors such as accessibility, topography, the climate, the availability of mineral and farming resources and, importantly, the history of colonialism and settlement.

The population density map (see page 13) shows a fairly simple pattern. Over 90 percent of Brazilians live in a zone along the Atlantic coast, which stretches inland for up to 500km. These coastal areas were the first to be colonized by Portuguese and other Europeans from the sixteenth century, and they have kept their economic and political importance to this day. Together, the Southeast and South regions are home to 57.6 percent of Brazilians, whereas the North and Centre-West, the country's two largest regions by area, contain only 13.3 percent of the population.

Curitiba, in the South, is a densely populated city, a magnet to migrants from poorer parts of Brazil.

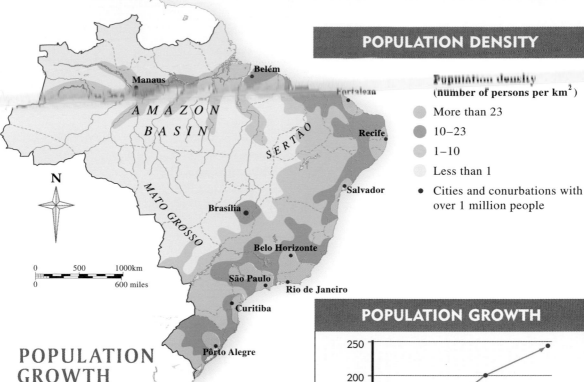

Population density
(number of persons per km^2)

- More than 23
- 10–23
- 1–10
- Less than 1
- Cities and conurbations with over 1 million people

POPULATION GROWTH

Brazil's population has tripled over the last 50 years (see graph). This growth is due to two processes: natural increase and large-scale immigration. However, the rate of increase has been slowing down, from 2.8 percent a year in the 1960s to 1.7 percent in the late 1990s. This is the result of social changes, which are leading to smaller families. Brazil is a Roman Catholic country, where contraception is not widely practiced and abortion is illegal. However, abortion is frequently resorted to, with estimates of 3 million–6 million abortions a year. Also, about 30 percent of Brazilian women of child-bearing age have been sterilized.

POPULATION STRUCTURE

Brazil is a young nation, with the "bottom-heavy" population structure of a Less Economically Developed Country (LEDC). Seventy percent of Brazilians are under 30 years old and one-third are under 15. This means that there is enormous pressure for jobs, new schools and welfare services. The present population growth means that some 1.5 million new jobs are needed every year. The proportion of people over 65 is only 3 percent, compared with 13 percent for Germany and other Western economies. The small number of old people shows the need for health improvements to increase people's life expectancy.

POPULATION GROWTH

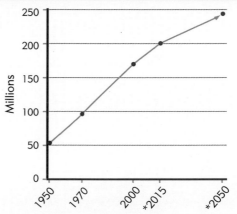

Sources: UN Population Division; *Geographical Digest*; UNDP   *=Estimates

POPULATION STRUCTURE

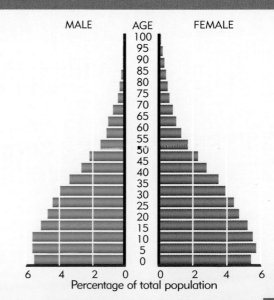

Source: *Understanding Global Issues: Brazil*
(UGI Ltd, 1999)

13

Rain-forest peoples still collect the red dye from the brasilwood tree, the tree that gave Brazil its name.

THE FIRST BRAZILIANS

The first people of Brazil were the Amerindians, who have lived on the continent for thousands of years. Unlike the Spanish *conquistadores* (conquerors) of the early sixteenth century, who discovered advanced native civilizations in Peru and Mexico, the Portuguese settlers of the early 1500s found far less sophisticated peoples when they

CASE STUDY
TERRA DO BRASIL

Early Portuguese traders named Brazil after the brasilwood tree, which can be used to produce a red dye. The Amerindians had long used the tree and its dye for many purposes, especially for painting their bodies. The Portuguese collected the wood and shipped its pulp to Europe, but the trade failed to lead to much success. However, it did give Brazil its name. *Brasa* in Portuguese means "embers" or "glowing coals," referring to the redness of the wood. Soon the colony was known as *terra do brasil*, meaning "land of the red dye-wood."

arrived in Brazil. The most advanced group were the Tupi Guarani, who lived in large coastal and riverbank villages growing manioc (cassava) and other crops, hunting, fishing and gathering fruits. But the Tupi Guarani had no stone buildings, no metal implements and only a basic administrative system. Inland from the coast other Amerindian peoples existed essentially as hunters and gatherers.

When the Portuguese arrived in the early 1500s, the number of native Amerindians in what is now Brazil was probably around 8 million, but away from the rich food supplies of the coast their densities were low. The colonists used the Amerindians as slaves. Others were killed by adventurers as they searched for gold, valuable wood and other riches. Many other Amerindians died from exposure to European infectious diseases, to which they were not immune.

Many Portuguese took Amerindian wives, which was the start of the process of miscegeneration (the intermixing of races) which has created such a diverse range of peoples in Brazil. Today there are probably around 200,000 Amerindians left in Brazil, and they are still under threat from developers. A number of organizations are campaigning for the protection of Amerindian land and cultural rights.

A MULTICULTURAL SOCIETY

Brazil's population is often described as a "melting pot" – always simmering and sometimes reaching boiling point. Brazilians are a mixture of many different races, including native Amerindians, European colonists, Africans and other immigrants. Between the sixteenth and nineteenth centuries, the Portuguese shipped millions of African slaves from West Africa to Brazil to work on their large plantations. Around 10 million had arrived in Brazil before slavery was finally abolished in 1888. Their descendants are an important element in modern Brazil's colorful mix of peoples, especially in the state of Bahia, often called "Africa in exile."

Not surprisingly, a large proportion of Brazilians are of Portuguese origin, but there are also large numbers of Italians, Spanish, Germans, Poles, Japanese and, more recently, Koreans and Middle Easterners. To these immigrants Brazil was, and still is, a land of opportunity.

Pure Amerindians make up less than 1 percent of the population. A larger proportion is made up of the *mamelucos*, the descendants of white Europeans and Amerindians. Other racial groups are the *cafuso* (those of Amerindian and African descent) and the *mulatto*, those of black and white descent.

The government's official view is that racial intolerance does not exist in Brazil. Many argue, however, that it is as deep-rooted as in parts of the United States and South Africa. "The whiter you are the richer you are" is a common Brazilian saying. Without doubt, the poorest rural and urban communities are the black *mulatto* and *cafuso*.

BELOW: Nineteenth-century immigration has given the South a distinctive European flavor, as shown in the architecture of the town of Blumenau, which has a strong German feel.

ABOVE: The Northeast was the heart of the African slave trade, a legacy left in the region's people and culture. This Bahian woman is dressed in traditional costume.

The rolling expanse of Mato Grosso state in the Brazilian Highlands.

Brazil can be divided into five main physical regions. In the north, the wild Guiana Highlands are shared with Venezuela, Guyana, Surinam and French Guiana. The highest mountain is Pico da Neblina (3,014m), near the Venezuelan border. The Guiana Highlands are the source of many large south-flowing tributaries of the Amazon River system and of others flowing north to Venezuela's Orinoco River.

The Brazilian Highlands, in the center of the country, form an enormous plateau of 200–2,000m in height, with abrupt escarpment edges and several higher mountain ranges. They form a huge watershed between the large, north-flowing Amazon tributaries and the tributaries of the Paraná and Paraguay Rivers. These river valleys slice through the plateau to form well-defined tablelands, called *chapadas*. Many impressive waterfalls occur along their steep edges. An important river that is confined to the Brazilian Highlands is the São Francisco. Starting in the state of Minas Gerais, it flows north before turning east to meet the Atlantic.

Between the Guiana Highlands and the Brazilian Highlands is the Amazon basin. Here, a vast lowland covered by rain forest stretches from the Andean foothills to the Atlantic. In the far west the lowland is 1,300km from north to south, but it narrows considerably eastwards where the Guiana and Brazilian Highlands are closer together. The Amazon

basin is a vast drainage system feeding the mighty Amazon River. It is four times larger than that of Africa's Zaire River and eleven times larger than the Mississippi drainage basin in the United States. Of the world's largest rivers, 10 are in the Amazon basin.

Brazil's other main lowland area is much smaller than Amazonia but is by no means small. It shares part of the flat upper Paraguay basin with Bolivia and Paraguay. This is now the Pantanal Wildlife Reserve (see page 21) which, with an area of 230,000km², is about the size of Utah.

The country's coastal belt, which stretches for over 7,400km, is bordered by the Atlantic and the eastern edge of the Brazilian Highlands. Mountainsides drop steeply to the sea, especially along the Great Escarpment, which extends from Pôrto Alegre to Salvador. The coastal belt is made up of pockets of lowland, many with natural harbors, which were important to the early settlement and economic development of Brazil.

These spectacular waterfalls are on the border of Brazil and northeastern Argentina, and 19km from the Paraguay border. The Iguaçu River begins near Curitiba, very close to the Atlantic. As it flows westwards, it is fed by about 30 tributaries before spectacularly plunging 80m down a crescent-shaped cliff. The waterfalls are one of the scenic wonders of South America and a major Brazilian tourist site. At times of peak flow, the water tumbles over 275 falls and cascades, with enough volume to fill six Olympic-sized swimming pools every second. But in some years rainfall is so slight that the river dries up altogether, as it did in May and June 1978.

The Iguaçu Falls are one of Brazil's main tourist attractions. They are also listed as one of the seven natural wonders of the world.

LANDSCAPE FEATURES

Fishermen with their traditional sailing boats, or *jangadas*, on the white sands of the tropical Northeast.

CLIMATE AND WATER RESOURCES

Brazil has a mostly warm and humid tropical climate, due to its position close to the Equator. In the west, Brazil's borders lie in the foothills of the Andes. But the country does not extend to the high peaks and ranges of these mountains, so no parts of Brazil have cold mountain climates.

FLOODING AND DROUGHT

Many parts of Brazil experience regular, often heavy rainfall, so water is one of its main natural resources. The country's greatest reservoir is the Amazon basin, which contains rivers that discharge a quarter of the world's fresh running water into the Atlantic. Much of the basin is flooded in the wet season (January to June) due to high rainfall. Snowmelt in the Andes also adds to the water levels. Some land in the basin is permanently flooded. Other land is above flood level. Floating homes and houses built on stilts are precautions against flooding.

A contrasting part of Brazil is the semi-desert found inland from the Northeast coast. Known as the *sertão*, it has been plagued by droughts for centuries, destroying crops and causing a heavy loss of life. The lack of water is the result of irregular wind systems failing to bring rain. But poor land management has also created this dry scrubland. The difficult climate of this region has driven thousands of people to seek a new life in other parts of Brazil, especially the large cities.

CLIMATIC REGIONS

Brazil has four main climate zones, which relate closely to the country's land height and distance from the Equator. The graphs opposite (page 19) show each region's temperature and rainfall statistics in places that are representative of the region.

AMAZONIA

Amazonia is always hot and wet. Temperatures hardly vary, with midday averages of 26.9°C. Local conditions produce less rainfall in the winter months, but there is no dry season. Heat and humidity make conditions unpleasant for visitors who are not used to the wet tropics (see Manaus graph opposite).

A lightning storm marks the onset of the rainy season in the Brazilian Highlands.

TROPICAL EAST COAST

The east coast has a warm tropical climate. Between May and August, temperatures are cooled by the Trade Winds blowing in from the Atlantic and can drop to around 22°C. December to April are the wettest months, but conditions are less humid than in Amazonia (see Rio de Janeiro graph).

THE BRAZILIAN HIGHLANDS

Most of the Brazilian Highlands have distinct wet and dry seasons. These are exaggerated in the Northeast, where long periods of drought are common. The Northeast has similar temperatures to those of Amazonia, but the daily ranges are greater (see Remansão graph).

NON-TROPICAL SOUTH

The non-tropical South has rainfall throughout the year, although marked temperature differences occur between winter and summer. Cold Antarctic air can lead to frosts and occasional snowfalls inland. This cooler climate attracted migrants from central Europe, especially Germans (see Pôrto Alegre graph).

TEMPERATURE AND RAINFALL

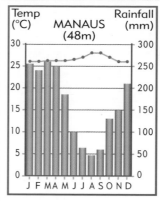

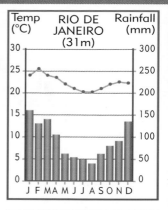

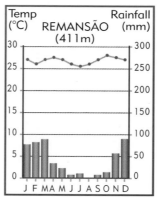

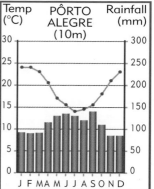

KEY:

Temp (°C)

Rainfall (mm)

Numbers in brackets show the city's height above sea level.

CLIMATE ZONES

AMAZONIA: rainy tropical

BRAZILIAN HIGHLANDS: wet and dry tropical

EAST COAST: tropical

SOUTH: warm, rainy, non-tropical

Jaguars and other magnificent animals of Brazil's rain forests are threatened by poaching and destruction of their habitat.

Little can be grown on the *sertão* of the Northeast and grazing animals struggle to find enough food.

VEGETATION AND ECOSYSTEMS

The great variety of vegetation types and ecosystems in Brazil is the result of the country's topography and climate, together with soil and drainage differences. Its ecosystems are easily disturbed and the country has many examples of ecosystems that have been changed or are now undergoing change by human as well as physical processes.

TROPICAL RAIN FOREST

Brazil's hot, wet Amazonian climate supports tropical rain forest. This is a complex ecosystem consisting of broadleaf evergreen trees which shed old leaves and grow new ones simultaneously. The great variety of tree species (estimated at 2,500 in each square kilometer) forms a layered canopy. The trees at the top of the canopy reach heights of 60m. Beneath them are a collection of lower-growing species, linked with lianas (vines) and covered with mosses and other plants. The light beneath the canopy is so dim that few plants can grow on the forest floor.

Animals and insects play a major part in the rain-forest ecosystem. They help to produce the biomass (organic matter) and to recycle nutrients in the rain forest. There are a vast number of mammals, reptiles, birds and freshwater fish living in the rain forest, of many different species. Of the many thousands of insect species already catalogued, an even greater number are thought likely to remain undiscovered.

SCRUBLANDS

There are two large scrubland regions in Brazil. A large part of Mato Grosso state, in the Centre-West, is wild and largely undeveloped bush country. It is often regarded as Brazil's frontier "wild west" country, where the dry and dusty landscape is home to poor farmers, Amerindians, miners, and rich ranchers with their hired hands (and often guns).

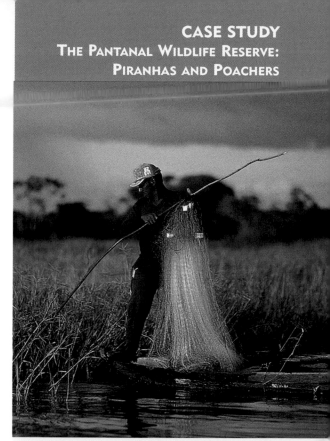

The Pantanal wetlands are rich in freshwater fish and other wildlife.

In the Northeast is the *sertão*, parched lands of brushwood and coarse grasses with large areas of *caatinga*, a vegetation of thick, impenetrable thorn shrubs and cacti. Brazil's scrublands are its most inhospitable environment.

THE ATLANTIC FORESTS

The thick forests that once covered the entire Atlantic coastal zone have been greatly reduced over the last 500 years, from an estimated 1.5 million km² in the sixteenth century to today's 10,000km². The forests have been cleared by agriculture, industry, lumbering and, above all, urbanization. The coniferous forests of the south are greatly reduced, especially the areas of the distinctive araucaria or paraná pine tree.

GRASSLANDS

Grasslands are found in Brazil's highland and plateau areas, where there is a distinct dry season. Known as *cerrados*, these grassy upland plains with areas of woodland are similar to the African savannas. They have been greatly altered as a result of human interference, especially burning to clear land for farming. This has reduced the habitat for wildlife such as foxes, rheas and wolves. Other grasslands are found in the temperate areas of the South. They are linked with the pampas of Uruguay and Argentina.

Brazil has many protected ecosystems, including over 350 national parks and wildlife reserves. One of the largest is the Pantanal, a huge swampy wetland with hundreds of species of freshwater fish, mammals, reptiles and birds. It is home to flesh-eating piranhas and the capybara, the world's largest rodent.

Tragically, the Pantanal's fragile ecosystem is under threat from river pollution caused by mining in Mato Grosso state and by illegal hunting. On top of pollution, the region is the target of internationally organized poaching groups, which supply the world's fashion industry with the pelts and skins of jaguars and caimans (crocodiles). Although illegal, the skins fetch high prices on the black market. Reduced numbers of caimans means the piranha population growth is uncontrolled, which in turn affects levels of fish and birds. Despite government bans, large numbers of colorful birds from the Pantanal end up in pet shops throughout the world.

Itaipú Dam is part of the world's largest hydroelectric power station.

Although Brazil is rich in many natural resources, it is short of fossil fuels – coal, oil and natural gas. Coal is mined near Pôrto Alegre, but most of the country's coal supplies are imported from the United States, mainly in the form of coke (produced from coal). Charcoal (produced from wood) is used in many of Brazil's manufacturing industries, but its use is heavily scrutinized by environmentalists because of its effect on forest reduction.

POWER AND ENERGY

Oil is in greatest demand because the country produces only one-fifth of its needs and relies heavily on imports. These imports have been reduced by the discoveries of oil and natural gas supplies off the coast between Salvador and Vitória. Substantial reserves have allowed Brazil to develop some of the best offshore oil technology anywhere in the world.

HYDROELECTRICITY

Brazil has vast supplies of water, which makes it one of the world's largest potential sources of hydroelectric power (HEP). The steep valleys and escarpment edges in the highland and plateau areas may not be suitable for river transport, but they do provide good sites for the dams and reservoirs of hydroelectric power stations. Hydropower now generates over 90 percent of Brazil's electricity.

CASE STUDY
THE ITAIPÚ DAM

In 2001, Itaipú Dam was the largest dam in the world. It is located on the Paraná River, close to Brazil's border with Paraguay. Fully operational in 1990, its 18 turbines are capable of producing 12.6 million kWh of energy, enough to supply the needs of southern Brazil and Paraguay. The dam was financed by foreign loans and is partly responsible for the country's huge national debts. It was one of the many giant projects of the military dictatorship, which ruled Brazil between 1964 and 1982. The amount of concrete used to build the dam would be enough to pave a two-lane highway across Europe, from Lisbon in Portugal to Moscow in Russia.

Many social and environmental issues result from Itaipú's 1,350km^2 reservoir. Over 40,000 families were forced off their land to make way for the reservoir, and the flooding involved a huge animal rescue program. The vast new reservoir has created a microclimate that may cause future problems. Critics have long argued that smaller schemes closer to the main economic centers would better serve Brazil's energy needs.

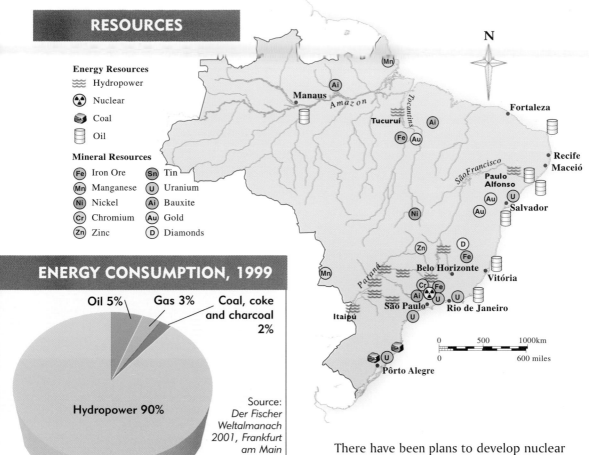

Energy Resources

- 〰 Hydropower
- ☢ Nuclear
- 🪨 Coal
- 🛢 Oil

Mineral Resources

- (Fe) Iron Ore
- (Mn) Manganese
- (Ni) Nickel
- (Cr) Chromium
- (Zn) Zinc
- (Sn) Tin
- (U) Uranium
- (Ai) Bauxite
- (Au) Gold
- (D) Diamonds

ENERGY CONSUMPTION, 1999

Oil 5%
Gas 3%
Coal, coke and charcoal 2%
Hydropower 90%

Source: *Der Fischer Weltalmanach 2001, Frankfurt am Main*

The Rio Paraná and its tributaries have hydroelectric power stations with reservoirs stretching for over 100km. The Rio São Francisco, which drains a large part of eastern Brazil, has large HEP stations near Belo Horizonte and at Paulo Alfonso, inland from Maceió.

A pickup truck stops to refuel with ethanol, a fuel made from sugarcane alcohol.

There have been plans to develop nuclear power but only one plant, near São Paulo, has been built.

ETHANOL: ALTERNATIVE ENERGY

Brazil has made important contributions to the search for alternative renewable energy sources. In 1975 it launched its *Pre-alcool* program, aimed at switching all motor vehicles from using gasoline to ethanol (a type of alcohol) made from sugarcane.

By 1980, Brazilian production of gasoline-only vehicles had been halted and replaced by engines burning either pure ethanol or gasohol, a mixture of gasoline and ethanol. This led to a marked improvement in pollution levels in cities like São Paulo, and it made Brazil less dependent on oil imports.

In recent years, the *Pre-alcool* program has suffered a series of setbacks linked to an increase in Brazil's own oil production and conflicts between sugarcane growers, distillers and the government over a fair price for ethanol.

MINERAL RESOURCES

Think of a mineral and Brazil probably mines it. The country's list of minerals is endless, from industrial ores and precious metals to gemstones, and huge areas of the country have not yet been surveyed. Brazil is a major world producer of iron ore, manganese, bauxite (for aluminum), nickel and tin. There are valuable deposits of uranium, thorium, and other minerals that are vital to today's high-tech industries.

"GOLD-RUSH" CULTURE

Brazil's economic growth is closely associated with mineral discoveries. Prospecting is said to be in the Brazilian blood. When gold was found in the Brazilian Highlands in the 1690s and diamonds in 1729, a great many people began searching. Fortune-hunters moved inland from the coast and were responsible for much of the country's early exploration and mapping. Many of the early mining settlements grew into rich colonial towns trading with São Paulo and Rio de Janeiro, from where precious minerals were shipped to Portugal. Between 1700 and 1800, nearly 1,000 tonnes of gold and 3 million carats of diamonds were exported from Brazil.

IRON ORE

The main concentration of early mining activity was in what became the state of Minas Gerais, its name meaning "general mines." This state still produces an incredible variety of minerals, but it is particularly famous for its iron ore. South and southwest of Belo Horizonte, the state capital, there are rugged mountains.

Brazil's early fortune-hunters found gold. In gratitude, they lavishly decorated many churches with the metal.

Prospecting can begin at an early age. A good find can change people's lives.

The most prominent summit is the jagged Itabirito, the shape of which is partly natural but now mainly the result of mining. As much as 70 percent of this peak is composed of iron ore. Around Belo Horizonte, the concentration of iron ore is reputed to be one of the world's highest. It is so great that in some of the city's suburbs, vehicles in neutral gear are drawn slowly uphill by magnetic force.

CASE STUDY
THE CARAJÁS PROJECT

The Carajás Project is situated in the Serra dos Carajás mountains in the state of Pará. This is where the world's largest-known iron-ore deposit is situated, which has Brazil's biggest concentration of minerals. Discovered in 1967, the region has an estimated 18 billion tonnes of iron ore reserves, which could supply the world for the next 500 years. Since the 1960s, massive strip mining has transformed tropical rain forest into huge areas of dusty, polluted landscape. Apart from iron ore, other minerals are mined, and activities such as logging, charcoal production and aluminum smelting add more pollution to the landscape.

The project is focused on a hydropower dam at Tucuruí on the Tocantins River. The idea is to develop an industrial zone 400,000km^2 in area – equivalent to the size of California. To help iron ore exports, a new railway through the rain forest links the mining town of Carajás with the modernized port of São Luis on the Atlantic coast. Plans for cities, highways, steelworks and agribusinesses make this Brazil's largest and most expensive project, costing many billions of dollars. Many people think it is unlikely to succeed, which is one of the reasons why the Brazilian government has encouraged private investment in the area.

THE NEW GARIMPEIROS

Today Brazil produces a large proportion of the world's gemstones, including diamonds, topazes, amethysts and emeralds, but it is gold that still captures the imagination. It was again discovered in Pará state in the 1970s. This led to a huge rush of *garimpeiros* (prospectors) from many parts of Brazil, but mainly from the poor Northeast. Open-cut mines (or strip mines) and shallow shafts are still dug by hand to form a massive lunar-like pit, where working conditions are grim and accidents frequent. Estimates vary as to the number of fortune-seekers but in the dry season, 60,000–100,000 might be involved.

Massive strip mining has transformed vast areas of the Brazilian landscape, much of which was once forest land.

AMAZONIA

Amazonia is a vast area of water and forest, a fragile ecosystem that is easily disrupted.

The Amazon rain forest, of which 60 percent belongs to Brazil, is a vast, complex and fragile ecosystem. It is home to one-tenth of the earth's entire plant and animal species and holds one-fifth of the earth's freshwater resources. It is like a massive "green lung" through which the earth breathes, which means that any interference has an impact on the rest of the world. The full effects of rain-forest destruction are not yet properly understood.

THE MIGHTY RIVER

From its source in the Peruvian Andes to its mouth at the Atlantic, the Amazon River flows over a distance of 6,440km, most of which is through the world's largest rain forest. The Amazon rain forest has an area of about 6.5 million km^2. Numerous huge tributaries add to the river's volume. Both the tributaries and the main river provide access to all the main settlements in Amazonia and have made those settlements possible as trading centers. The city of Manaus lies 1,600km inland, close to where the Negro tributary joins the main river. The city is a collection and distribution center for the towns and villages along the river and is served by oceangoing liners.

The Amazon River discharges 4.5 trillion gallons of water a day into the Atlantic, an amount capable of supplying every US household for six months. The river system also carries immense amounts of sediment from its source to the sea, but the flow is too strong for a true delta to form. Instead, the Amazon reaches the sea in a complicated system of channels and islands. The largest of these islands, Marajó, is the size of Switzerland. At the river's mouth, the north and south banks are farther apart than the distance between London and Paris.

THE RUBBER TRADE

Compared with the rest of Brazil, Amazonia was economically poor until commercial tapping of the rubber tree began in the nineteenth century. The Amerindians had been harvesting the latex from the rubber tree for hundreds of years,

The large city of Belém, at the mouth of the Amazon, is the region's main port. Both Belém and Manaus, a city in the heart of Amazonia, grew rich on the products of the forest.

making shoes and waterproof containers. They called the tree *cahuchu*, meaning "weeping tree," from the drops of latex that oozed from the bark. As manufacturers in the United States and Europe discovered how to make products from the rubber such as raincoats, hoses and shoes, the rubber industry grew. At first all the rubber came from the wild. Harvesting was difficult because the rubber tree grows on its own and trees are often spaced far apart in the rain forest.

In the early twentieth century, the invention of the automobile and rubber tires created a high demand for rubber, which led to a rapid growth in Amazonia's population as people moved in to make their fortune. By 1910, Brazil was supplying 88 percent of the world's rubber, controlled from Belém and Manaus by rich rubber barons. But the boom was short-lived. By 1911 Brazil was unable to compete with the huge rubber plantations of Malaya, developed from seeds smuggled out of Amazonia.

Attempts to establish rubber plantations in Amazonia, such as the Henry Ford project in the Tapajós Valley, have ended in failure. This project, which started in 1928, involved extensive forest clearance and the rubber trees eventually died from disease brought on by soil exhaustion – a lesson still to be learned in Amazonia. The project was sold to the Brazilian government in 1945. There are still rubber tappers in the forest and special reserves protect the trees. Output, however, is a pale reflection of rubber's boom years.

Rubber tappers still work in the rain forest, but they may tap from trees in extractive reserves, such as this one in the state of Acre.

DEVELOPMENT IN AMAZONIA

Over the last 100 years, numerous attempts have been made to open up the Amazon's frontiers to make the most of what was seen as a valuable resource going to waste. The government cooperated with foreign companies on a variety of projects. There were three main objectives to these projects:

1. To populate some of Brazil's northern and western frontiers in order to strengthen its control over disputed territories.
2. To encourage landless peasant farmers to inhabit the region.
3. To search for and exploit minerals and other resources.

CASE STUDY
THE TRANS-AMAZONIA HIGHWAY

The Trans-Amazonia Highway (see map on page 11), was begun in the 1960s. It crosses southern Amazonia from the Atlantic (via the Belém-Brasília highway) to the Peruvian border, a distance of 5,400km. It is another of Brazil's grand and expensive schemes, part of the plan to open up Amazonia and attract people from the dry Northeast region. The highway construction has been much criticized for causing extensive forest destruction and the eviction of Amerindians. Only a small section is asphalted, and both weather erosion and underuse have meant it is deteriorating rapidly.

The construction of the Trans-Amazonia Highway destroyed large areas of forest.

ROAD BUILDING

After the 1950s, a large program of road building took place in Brazil. In Amazonia the aim was to encourage people to settle and develop the region. But road building through the Amazon, such as the Trans-Amazonia Highway, has destroyed huge swaths of forest, sometimes for little purpose. Many roads are unfinished or poorly maintained and have been reduced to potholes and quagmires.

LAND CLEARANCE

Clearing land for cultivation has also been a failure. The rain forest appears to be supported by fertile soils, but this is not true. The soil relies on the remains of plants and animals for nutrition, so when vegetation is cleared for farming, the soils become thin and infertile within two to three years and few crops can be grown. The Amerindians understand this important relationship and have special ways of farming the land (see page 30). But the migrants who move to Amazonia from places like the Northeast do not. A few years after moving to the region and clearing a plot of land, many find that they can grow little food. The migrants often find that they have moved from one rural poverty trap to another.

CATTLE RANCHES

Both migrant farmers and Amerindians have had to compete with large companies who ruthlessly displace people and use their land for vast cattle ranches. Ecologists agree that the conversion of rain forest to grazing land for animals is the worst possible use of the land. Toxic weeds are a problem to animals and the only way to get rid of the weeds is by burning, which causes air pollution and disturbs the ecosystem. Most ranches are abandoned after five years, leaving a totally degraded landscape.

DAM BUILDING

The building of dams and the creation of huge reservoirs for hydroelectric power stations have damaged Amazonia's ecology. As forest

Hundreds of thousands of landless peasant families like these have moved into Amazonia from other parts of Brazil, looking for a better life.

vegetation is flooded, it decomposes, rots, and is continuously washed into the reservoirs, emitting large amounts of carbon dioxide and methane. These are two important greenhouse gases. Calculations show that the Turcuruí reservoir, part of the Carajás Project in Pará state, has had 60 percent more impact on global warming than a coal-fired power station generating the same amount of energy.

Other damage from dam building is caused by the workers themselves. Dam construction requires huge amounts of labor. Migrant laborers come from all parts of Brazil. They are housed in temporary accommodation, with bars and brothels. Such concentrations of people can lead to health hazards including the spread of tuberculosis, AIDS and sexually transmitted diseases.

Many of the large-scale projects to develop Amazonia have been expensive failures, and most have resulted in the disruption of the rain-forest ecosystem and the loss of Amerindian homelands.

In the state of Acre, large expanses of forest have been cleared for cattle pasture. Only the valuable Brazil nut trees have been spared.

AMERINDIANS

The Amerindian groups have been the main victims of rain-forest destruction, which has increasingly destroyed their land and their livelihood. These are the people who really understand the forest, live in harmony with the ecosystem and could teach the rest of the world how to protect the environment.

SUBSISTENCE ECONOMIES

The Amerindians use the forest's resources in two ways: basic hunting and gathering, and the more advanced farming. This is a type of subsistence economy, where they only take from the rain forest what they need themselves. Hunting and gathering is based on the great variety of food available in the rain forest – animal, plant and insect life. This lifestyle is a wandering or nomadic existence in which men hunt and women gather foods from the forest.

Amerindian farming is also known as "shifting cultivation." After clearing a patch of forest by cutting and burning away the vegetation (leaving food-providing trees such as the banana and kola nut), the ashes are dug into the soil as a fertilizer. A variety of crops are grown, such as yams and manioc, as well as beans, pumpkins and tobacco. Without the vegetation cover and forest nutrients, the soil loses its fertility after two or three years, so

A small forest clearing is the first stage in subsistence cultivation.

the farmers move on to clear a new plot. The land they have abandoned is left fallow for about 10 years to allow the growth of secondary forest. Many rain-forest dwellers prefer to work these areas rather than primary forest, because they are easier to clear. This relieves pressure on the primary forest and minimizes its destruction.

Shifting cultivation allows the forest to recover after its soil has been used for growing crops. In contrast, recent peasant migrants to Amazonia have used "slash-and-burn" techniques to clear the land, where the soil is not allowed to recover its fertility and suffers from erosion. These migrants practice what is known as a "robber economy" – the over-exploitation of renewable resources.

PROTECTING THE AMERINDIANS

The Brazilian Amerindians are protected by FUNAI, the government Amerindians Agency. Some 850,000km^2 (10 percent of Brazil's territory) has been set aside as reservation land where, technically, they are free to practice their traditional lifestyles. However, the Amerindians continue to suffer from ruthless land encroachment and dispossession

CASE STUDY
FOREST MEDICINE

Living as part of the forest ecosystem, the Amerindians have a detailed knowledge of the various properties and uses of plants. Scientific investigation has shown that many hundreds of species have important medicinal uses. In fact, one in four of the ingredients found in a Western drugstore come from the leaves, roots, fruits and barks of forest plants. Tribal shamans, whose knowledge is handed down orally, know of forest plants that can help cure a great variety of medical conditions. If the forest and the Amerindians are wiped out, this knowledge will disappear.

Medicinal plants and extracts from the forest can be found for sale in most Brazilian markets.

by brute force. The now-famous Yanomami, an Amerindian group discovered in Roraima in 1973, were people with traditional ways forced to confront the modern age. The transition was not easy. Today their numbers have been greatly reduced by the influx of lumber companies and mineral speculators.

Amerindians use the forest resources carefully. This man has collected vines for busket-making in the rain forest near Manaus.

FAIR TRADE

There are some examples of fair dealing with the Amerindians, however. The Kayapo harvest Brazil nuts for the British company The Body Shop. Oil from the nuts is used in cosmetics and the Amerindians are paid a suitable wage for their work. In Germany, Spain and Portugal, other "green-conscious" companies have fair trading relationships with the Amerindians. Their products are found in many department stores and drugstores.

AGRICULTURE

Harvesting the coffee cherry depends on labor-intensive hand-picking methods.

Brazil is one of the world's most important farming countries. Agriculture employs a quarter of the working population and provides 40 percent of exports. The most important product is coffee. Brazil is the world's leading producer and exporter of coffee. On the world market, the coffee industry is second only to the oil industry in importance and value, with over 25 million people around the world gaining their living from its production and sale.

CASE STUDY
COFFEE

Coffee plantations occupy some 2.4 million hectares of Brazil. São Paulo, Minas Gerais and Paraná are the major coffee-producing states, where a combination of suitable landscape, climate and rich soil provide ideal conditions for the crop.

The coffee bean is the seed of the coffee tree. It grows inside a fruit, called a "cherry," and develops over a period of six to nine months. The trees are planted in rows on well-drained hillsides, mostly at altitudes of between 300 and 1,000m. The cherries need maximum sunshine to ripen and are sensitive to high wind, drought and sudden falls in temperature. Heavy frosts ruined large harvests in 1994 and output was reduced in 2001 by prolonged water shortage. Both years resulted in sharp rises in coffee prices. The price of coffee is controlled by the Brazilian Coffee Institute by regulating the amount of coffee grown and sold on the world market each year. Coffee has important economic and political value in world trade transactions.

Coffee estates are labor intensive, especially at harvest time. Cherries on the same bush ripen at different times, which means that harvesting has to be done by hand and each bush requires several visits by pickers. Once the cherries have been collected, the bean must be separated from its outer pulp then dried and roasted. There are a number of roasting procedures to determine the coffee's flavor, aroma and strength. These processes, together with storage, packaging and shipment, explain the high market cost of coffee.

Brazil's other major export crops are sugar, cocoa, soybeans and maize (corn). Thanks to its climate, almost every kind of fruit is grown, from tropical to temperate varieties. The enormous output of citrus fruit is exported mainly as concentrated juice. A variety of nuts and spices also find their way to the shelves of the world's supermarkets.

CASH CROPS AND PLANTATIONS

From the early days of colonialism, Brazilian agriculture has been based on the production of one cash crop for export, beginning with sugarcane. Other crops were cotton, cocoa,

Many landless families travel in search of farm work, such as the tending and harvesting of field crops.

rubber and coffee. These crops were, and in some states still are, grown on plantations. Before the twentieth century, the plantations used slave labor on large estates, called *fazendas*. Today, the same estates employ temporary workers on short-term contracts. Many people, known as *caboclos*, travel the Brazilian countryside in search of seasonal jobs, moving from one plantation after another as they follow the work available.

MIGRANT WORKERS

For many rural workers, this seasonal migration is a necessity. Brazil is a country of extreme agricultural inequality, with many thousands of landless families struggling to make a living. According to the World Bank, 43 percent of the country's farmed land belongs to only 0.3 percent of landowners, many of which are now multinational companies. Government land reform and redistribution movements have had little effect in changing land ownership since their main action has been to provide land in Amazonia, where farming methods have not been successful.

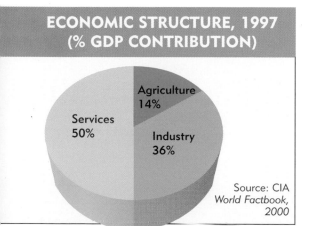

ECONOMIC STRUCTURE, 1997 (% GDP CONTRIBUTION)

Agriculture 14%
Services 50%
Industry 36%

Source: CIA *World Factbook*, 2000

AGRICULTURE

Manaus
Recife
Salvador
Belo Horizonte
São Paulo
Rio de Janeiro
Pôrto Alegre

N

0   500   1000km
0   600 miles

● **Plantation farming:** cocoa, cotton, tobacco and sugar

○ **Plantations and arable:** coffee, sugar cane and cereals

● **Extensive and intensive farming:** cattle, sheep, soya, grains, fruits and vegetables

● **Tropical forest:** subsistence farming and ranching

○ **Extensive farming:** cattle and pigs

● Rubber

Despite some mechanization, sugarcane is a labor-intensive crop that uses farming methods little different from those of colonial times.

THE NORTHEAST: SUGAR, COCOA AND COLONIALISM

The Northeast is Brazil's problem region, characterized by poverty, underemployment, and loss of people through migration. One of the main reasons why the region is unable to support its population is related to the unequal distribution of land. The region is divided between a relatively small number of extremely rich landowners and masses of poor, illiterate farmworkers, most of whom have no land at all. This situation is the survival of a system that dates from colonial times.

THE COLONIAL SYSTEM
The Northeast was the first part of Brazil to be settled by Europeans. They introduced the plantation system and the early landowners grew rich on crops grown for export, first

sugarcane in the sixteenth century and later cocoa in the 1850s. The sugar empires depended entirely on African slave labor, while cocoa relied on grossly underpaid and landless farm laborers. Technically these laborers were "wage slaves," like the majority of rural workers in the Northeast today. "Without land you are nothing" is a Northeast saying.

PLANTATIONS AND POVERTY
The ownership of massive estates by a powerful minority is responsible for the Northeast's continuing poverty. The *fazendeiros* (estate owners) have become Brazil's ruling class once again. They have a strong influence on the governments of the Northeast states and, as a result, with the federal government in Brasília. Many estate owners are unprepared to part with their land or agree to agrarian reform. Instead they support a system that pays very low wages for long hours and often dangerous working conditions, and one that hires and fires workforces at will.

SUGAR AND COCOA
The Northeast's coastal areas, with their tropical temperatures and high rainfall levels, are well suited to cultivation of sugarcane and cocoa, which employs most of the region's rural workers. Both crops require minimal levels of technology but a large supply of unskilled labor. Plantations have replaced much of the original coastal rain forest, which now only exists in tiny pockets. However, the plantations' soil has been impoverished as a result of monoculture – the cultivation of the same crop on the same piece of land – which quickly uses up nutrients.

Brazil is the world's largest producer of sugar, accounting for 13 percent of the global total. The refined product is exported throughout the world with Russia, Nigeria and Middle Eastern countries being the largest markets. The country's own demand for sugar has also increased. This is linked to the growth in soft drink and confectionery products, as well as the production of ethanol (see page 23). Outside the Northeast, sugarcane is also important in parts of the South and Southeast.

Although cocoa beans are still an important crop in the Northeast, the world demand for chocolate made from cocoa beans has fallen. This has resulted in lower prices for cocoa, which have forced landowners to reduce their output and cut the number of rural jobs. The main chocolate-consuming countries are the United States and those of Western Europe, such as Germany, Belgium, the Netherlands and the United Kingdom. The trade is controlled by multinational companies (see page 39). Cheaper substitutes for cocoa, including chopped cabbage and pig's blood, are now used in "chocolate" products instead of cocoa beans. On top of reduced world demand for the beans, Brazil's cocoa zone is plagued by a fungus disease called "witches'-broom," which frequently destroys entire plantations.

THE BACKLANDS

Inland from the coast is the *sertão*, which covers a large area of the Northeast. This barren region has become arid and infertile as a result of drought and land mismanagement, including overgrazing. Many thousands of people have died over the years due to starvation and disease. Better-quality lands, such as those found in some of the river valleys, have been claimed by powerful cattle barons. The rest of the population has been

The Northeast's tropical climate is ideal for growing citrus fruits.

pushed into less favorable areas and drought regularly forces them to seek refuge in the coastal cities. They are known as the *flagelados*, the "scourged ones," and are Brazil's most socially destitute and desperate victims of poverty.

Despite the social and economic problems of the Northeast, fish is one foodstuff the region has in abundance.

THE SOUTH: RANCHES AND VINEYARDS

No part of Brazil is more different from the Northeast than the country's South region. Since most of the South lies below the Tropic of Capricorn it has four better-marked seasons, with frosts and occasional snowfalls in winter. This climate helped to attract large numbers of immigrants from Italy, Germany, Poland and Russia. They give the region a distinctive European character, especially in the country towns and villages, which have kept many of their European customs, traditions and, in places, dialects merged with Portuguese (see case study below).

INTENSIVE AND EXTENSIVE FARMING

Two distinctive farming economies exist in the South, influenced by physical conditions. Along the coast, particularly in the state of Santa Catarina, intensive farming is practiced on family-run farms. The farms produce a variety of grains, fruits (including vines) and vegetables, and raise cattle, sheep, pigs and

poultry. This mixed farming system greatly differs from the monoculture of Brazil's plantation system. Farming cycles, particularly harvests, are celebrated with colorful festivals based on European customs.

CASE STUDY
EUROPEAN CULTURE: VINEYARDS AND BREWERIES

Inside a cellar of a major winery in Rio Grande do Sul.

Italian immigrants first introduced vines to the valleys and coastal hillsides of Rio Grande do Sul at the end of the nineteenth century. Today this is where 90 percent of Brazilian wine is produced. The villages and small farms of the area, with their cheeses, salamis, pastas and wine cellars, retain the air of Italy about them. The introduction of Californian and other grape varieties from Europe has improved the quality of Brazil's wines, which are finding new markets throughout the world.

German immigrants also brought beer-making skills to the South and were responsible for the region's breweries. The annual *Oktoberfest*, a beer festival modeled on the original festival in Munich, is held in the town of Blumenau every year and is now the second-largest festival in Brazil, after the Rio Carnival. Visits by German orchestras, folk-dancing displays and German food make sure German culture is preserved in the region.

The South's temperate grasslands are ideal for grazing cattle.

In the South, the proud *gauchos* retain their culture and traditions.

In contrast, the rolling inland grasslands of the South are areas of extensive crop and animal farming. Together with parts of São Paulo state they form what is called Brazil's "breadbasket," growing wheat, maize, rice and soybeans. They also have the country's largest cattle ranches and sheep populations. These temperate grasslands are some of the leading areas of commercial grazing in the world. The climate and rich grasses allow year-round grazing, and the animals are also fed on grains and other fodder crops.

Brazil is the world's fourth-largest beef producer, with the South having a quarter of the country's estimated 150 million head of cattle. However, the region is losing this position to the Southeast and Centre-West, where interbreeding with zebus (a species of humped oxen) and Angolan stock has produced cattle that are better at surviving the drier conditions of the Brazilian Highlands. A growing number of the South's former ranches are now dominated by endless expanses of soybean crops which, ironically, are exported to feed European cattle.

The South American cowboy, the *gaucho*, is a very common sight in Brazil's South, as in other cattle farming areas in Brazil. *Gauchos* roam the grasslands with large numbers of cattle or sheep, helping to provide Brazil with meat, leather and wool for its textile industries. One of the main centers of *gaucho* traditions is Santana do Livramento, on the border with Uruguay. Here a unique culture has developed, a mixture of Portuguese and Spanish, together with Italian and German lifestyles.

Ranching is so important to Brazil that it has developed its own distinctive festivals, many of which originated in the *sertão* lands of the Northeast. Rodeos are common gatherings in the cattle towns, with one of the most important held at Uruguaiana, on the Argentine border. The riding and other skilled events of the rodeo attract competitors from all over Brazil, Uruguay and Argentina. Like North American cowboys, some are professionals, earning a living by moving from one event to another.

37

A steelworks near São Paulo. Iron and steel-making are Brazil's major heavy industries.

Brazil is a newly industrializing country (NIC) with a wealthier economy than any other South American country. An important characteristic of an NIC is the growth of its manufacturing industry and products for export. Essentially an agricultural economy up until the mid-twentieth century, Brazil now has an economy where industry is of increasing importance. Manufactured goods today account for more than two-thirds of total exports.

DEVELOPMENT POLICIES

The change from agriculture to manufacturing in Brazil's economy is the result of deliberate government policy. The policy supports two strategies. The first is the development of its export market, where products are sold abroad. The second is the development of manufacturing for the country's own market, especially the production of consumer goods. The government restricts the import of certain goods from abroad, greatly benefiting Brazil's domestic industries.

INDUSTRIALIZATION IN THE SOUTHEAST

Brazil's steel and other mineral-based industries, transport equipment, petrochemicals, machinery and food products

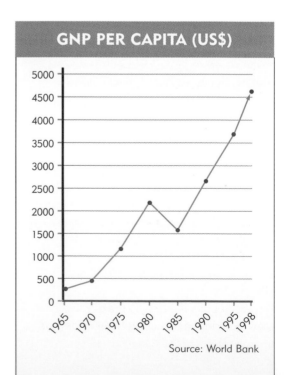

GNP PER CAPITA (US$)

Source: World Bank

Most heavy industrial products are exported through the port of Santos, the closest port to São Paulo.

have played major roles in its economic expansion. The country's most industrialized region is the Southeast, especially the "industrial triangle" formed by the huge conurbations of São Paulo, Rio de Janeiro and Belo Horizonte. São Paulo state has about 50 percent of Brazilian industry and the city is South America's largest industrial center.

THE MULTINATIONALS

São Paulo is the headquarters for most of the foreign multinational companies that control a large part of Brazilian industry. Their growth is due to the government policy of reducing state control of industry and increasing privatization and foreign investment. Multinational companies have been able to profit from Brazil's huge foreign debt (see page 54) and its repayments to global institutions. In 1999, 14 of Brazil's 20 largest companies in terms of sales revenue were owned by foreign companies. They include oil consortiums such as Shell, Texaco and Esso; Carrefour (supermarkets); Nestlé (food products); Gessy Lever (hygiene products) and most of the world's automobile companies.

THE AUTOMOBILE INDUSTRY

The automobile industry is Brazil's top manufacturing sector in terms of sales figures.

Although it began an just a few assembly plants in the early twentieth century, the industry currently produces an average of 1 million vehicles a year. They are built using components made in Brazil rather than imported parts. The country ranks tenth among the world's motor vehicle producers, and General Motors, Ford, Fiat, Toyota, Volkswagen and Mercedes-Benz all have production and assembly plants in the country. In addition to cars and trucks, there is an important output of tractors and other agricultural vehicles, motorcycles and railway parts.

AIRCRAFT AND SPACE RESEARCH

Brazilians were among the pioneers of early aviation, but their aircraft industry only really began 25 years ago. It has rapidly grown to become the sixth-largest in the world. The main company, Embraer, exports commercial and military aircraft throughout the world. The company is also leading the move towards full jet travel on the country's air routes.

Brazil's aerospace industry has also seen rapid growth, which has led to remote surveillance and satellite monitoring of the country's huge territory. This plays an important role in environmental protection, especially in Amazonia and other sparsely populated areas.

Workers at the Embraer aircraft factory put the finishing touches to a new passenger jet.

TYPES OF TRANSPORT BY JOURNEY, 2000

Air 3.5%   Water 3%

Rail 1.5%

Road 92%

Source:
Brazil
Information
Center

CASE STUDY
BRAZILIAN BUS JOURNEYS

Bus journeys in Brazil can be lengthy, often needing overnight stops. This is where the *rodoviaria*, or bus terminal, plays an important role. Usually located on the outskirts of a city, it is much more than a busy bus station. As well as dealing with timetables and tickets, it is also a retail, services, and leisure center, catering to the needs of travelers whose journeys can last a number of days and nights. Brazilian bus services are mostly efficient and of high quality. They belong to hundreds of private companies and connect all inhabited parts of the country, even where road surfaces are little more than rural tracks. However, the poor quality of transport in its most isolated areas illustrates that Brazil is a developing country.

A bustling bus station in Brasília.

Modern subway systems, like this one in São Paulo, try to ease traffic congestion in the city by encouraging people to take public transport instead of the car.

TRANSPORT

Brazil's vast size and endless stretches of rain forest, *sertão* and *cerrado* make many land journeys long and difficult. For those who can afford it, air travel is the most efficient means of travel, but most Brazilians rely on the bus or, in Amazonia, the river boats.

ROADS

A large amount of money is spent on Brazilian roads, which transport over 90 percent of the country's population and goods. There are over 1.6 million km of roads, but only some 7 percent are paved, making driving conditions difficult in wet weather. The densest network (see map page 11) is in the Southeast region, where modern motorways link São Paulo, Rio de Janeiro, Belo Horizonte and Brasília. The busiest stretch of highway is that linking São Paulo with the port of Santos.

Practically all the state capitals are linked by paved roads and many have modern expressways. But traffic is a huge problem in and around the large conurbations, where routes are constantly clogged with cars, trucks and buses. Exhaust fumes pollute the air and São Paulo, with its added industrial toxins, is one of the world's most polluted cities.

RAILWAYS

Like the road network, the main railway network is also in the Southeast (see map page 11), but in proportion to the roads it is relatively small. Most of the railway lines were built in the nineteenth century to carry minerals and agricultural produce to the ports for export. There is still an extensive freight network, but passenger services are limited, slow and more expensive than buses. The busiest route is the luxury night service between São Paulo and Rio de Janeiro. Some lines are specifically aimed at tourists. They use steam-powered trains on routes through scenic mountains and colonial countrysides.

AIR TRAVEL

Brazil has one of the largest internal air networks in the world, with the busiest route, São Paulo to Rio de Janeiro, operating a daily shuttle service. As well as the major city airports, every state capital has an airport or airfield where air taxis, or "teco-teco" flights, are popular with business people. As in other countries with large, remote areas, air services are often social and medical lifelines.

RIVER BOATS

Tourists can see the Amazon from the deck of a cruise ship, but most Brazilians are dependent on the slow and uncomfortable steamers that travel between the various ferryboat terminals. A two-hour air journey between Belém and Manaus increases to four to five days by river. Traveling by river boat is monotonous, painstaking and lacking all but the most basic facilities. A hammock on deck is more comfortable than a crowded and poorly ventilated cabin.

The Amazon river ports are always scenes of colorful activity.

TIME TO BRASÍLIA (HOURS)

CITY	BY AIR	BY BUS
Belo Horizonte	1.00	12
São Paulo	1.25	16
Rio de Janeiro	1.25	20
Pôrto Alegre	2.20	33
Manaus	2.30	35
Foz do Iguaçu	3.25	28

Source: Brazil Information Center

URBAN BRAZIL

Olinda (in the foreground) and Recife (behind) show both historical and modern development. Olinda grew wealthy from sugar in colonial times.

Brazil has a great variety of towns and cities, ranging from "pioneer" towns in Amazonia and Mato Grosso state to massive conurbations. The variety of settlements is partly due to the physical size and diversity of the country, but it is also due to Brazil's history and the origins of its immigrants.

COLONIAL TOWNS

Brazil's earliest towns grew from trading posts along the Atlantic and inland centers of prospecting, which depended on the coast for export links with Europe. The construction of forts at places like Recife, Salvador and Rio de Janeiro provided centers for urban growth.

The plan and architecture of these colonial towns were greatly influenced by the Portuguese settlers, and many of these centers, particularly in the Northeast and Minas Gerais, are now protected heritage sites. However, they are surrounded by largely unplanned modern urban sprawl.

URBANIZATION

From the middle of the nineteenth century, many of Brazil's historic towns were altered by a rapid process of urbanization. The main cause of this growth was immigration. Urbanization continues to the present day with 81 percent of the country's population classified as living in towns and cities (see graph on page 43). The annual urban growth rate is 3 percent, which means that many Brazilian cities will double their population in a few decades.

Population figures are difficult to calculate because there are many thousands, especially

BRAZIL'S LARGEST CITIES, 1999

	Population (millions)
São Paulo	16.6
Rio de Janeiro	10.3
Belo Horizonte	4.6
Salvador	3.1
Fortaleza	2.3

Source: *Der Fischer Weltalmanach 2001, Frankfurt am Main*

Poor migrants with large families swell the numbers in Brazil's big cities.

Traffic congestion in São Paulo is just one of the problems caused by rural-urban migration.

those living in *favela* districts (slums), who are not on urban registers. This means that population totals could possibly be doubled.

RURAL-URBAN MIGRATION

The movement of people from the countryside to the cities is a major cause of urbanization. Most migrants head for the Southeast, which dominates Brazil's economy. The "pull factors," or attractions, are promises of better economic and social lifestyles. Most migrants come from the Northeast, where the "push factor" is poverty. Rural migrants have large families, bringing even more people to the cities.

Urban growth brings other problems. Housing, transport and services cannot cope with the sheer volume of newcomers, traffic jams cause chaos, and air pollution is often life-threatening. Many wealthier people are moving out of Brazil's large cities to set up homes and business in smaller towns, which offer a better quality of life.

CASE STUDY
BAHIA – THE "PUSH FACTORS"

Poverty and a low quality of life force people to leave the Northeast. In Bahia state, only 18 out of 415 cities have basic sanitation, and out of every 1,000 infants, 43 do not survive their first year. About 40 percent of Bahia's schools are closed due to lack of funds and half the state's population is illiterate. The number of unemployed is 30 percent of the workforce. The government has been unable to curb the drift to the Southeast of those in search of a living wage.

URBAN POPULATION

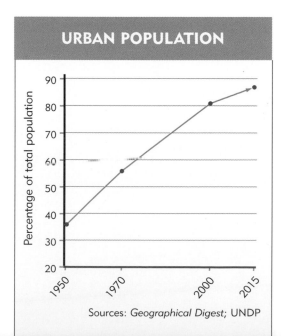

Sources: *Geographical Digest*; UNDP

ABOVE: Busy beaches and boulevards are some of the characteristics of Rio de Janeiro.

RIO DE JANEIRO AND SÃO PAULO – THE "URBAN GIANTS"

RIO DE JANEIRO ("RIO")

In January 1502, Portuguese explorers visited Guanabara Bay. Mistaking it for a river, they called it Rio de Janeiro, "River of January." Had they sailed farther into the bay they would have discovered that it forms a huge natural harbor, one of the largest, safest and most beautiful in the world. The city of Rio spreads around the irregular shores of this great harbor, which is a complex of rocky peninsulas, sheltered havens, extensive beaches, dome-shaped mountains and palm-fringed islands. The shape of the harbor makes Rio one of the world's most dramatically sited cities, but also one of the most difficult in terms of urban planning.

Rio began its history as a fortified Portuguese outpost but grew to prominence as the export port for the mineral wealth and agricultural produce of the inland areas. In 1763, the city replaced Salvador as Brazil's capital, and for a short time in the nineteenth century it became capital of the entire Portuguese Empire, including Portugal itself. Many buildings survive from the city's colonial days.

BELOW: Architectural giants cramp older buildings in São Paulo, Brazil's economic powerhouse.

Today Rio is famous for its intense and varied cultural life. It is said that the city's main industry is the pursuit of pleasure, but this ignores its role as a major manufacturing, services and financial center. The city lost its capital status to Brasília in 1960 but it has not lost its urban attractions. There are wealthy districts of luxury apartment blocks and expensive shopping boulevards on a par with those in European and North American cities. The image of Rio's "bright lights" is a magnet to many Brazilian migrants, thousands of whom find themselves living in one of the many *favelas* that crowd the swampy coastal areas and steep mountain sides. Towering over the city, on the 709m-high Corcovado mountain, is a huge statue of Christ. There is argument as to whether he guards an urban Garden of Eden or a "concrete jungle."

SÃO PAULO

The people of São Paulo often comment that whereas Rio's *Cariocas* are fond of enjoying themselves, they, the *Paulistas*, are dedicated to enterprise and hard work. There is certainly a different atmosphere in what is Brazil's largest city and economic powerhouse. Over 20,000 industrial plants of all types and sizes employing 600,000 workers are concentrated in the city and its surrounding towns. São Paulo is also the major financial center of Brazil, with nearly 2,000 banking agencies.

The city's rapid growth and high-rise development have obliterated almost everything of old São Paulo, which was founded by Portuguese Jesuit priests in 1554. They chose a plateau site for their mission at 760m above sea level but only 72km from the coast. Here a number of river valleys fanned into the interior. *Bandeirantes*, adventurers and fortune-hunters who explored the Brazilian hinterland in the fifteenth and sixteenth centuries, also used the site as a base. Some of the modern expressways radiating from São Paulo follow routes opened up by the *bandeirantes* and *tropeiros* (cattle drovers).

The old colonial settlement was transformed by the coffee boom of the late nineteenth century, which brought massive immigration. São Paulo became a migrant city, which it continues to be today. The port of Santos grew with São Paulo to become the world's largest coffee-exporting port. It now serves the industries of the Southeast with some of the most modern dockside installations in South America.

From the older central districts, São Paulo spreads in all directions like an endless urban jungle of high-rise concrete, steel and glass buildings, carved through by highways, boulevards, viaducts and railway tracks. Close to the city center are the wealthy villas of the rich, enclosed by lush gardens. These are the homes of those who made São Paulo rich. A visit to a *favela* shows a very different side of life in the city.

The lush watered gardens of São Paulo's wealthy are a sharp contrast to the city's *favelas*.

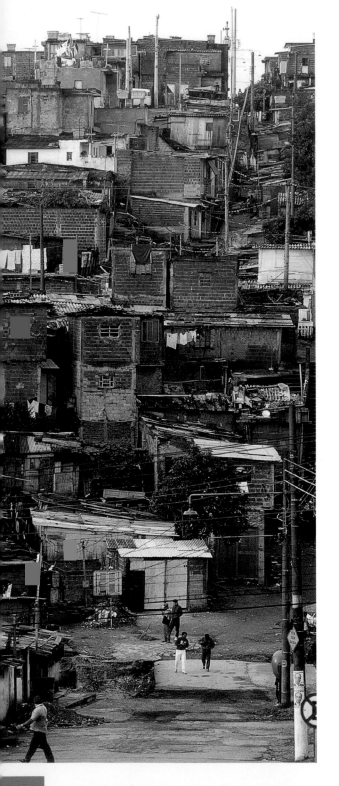

Rio has some of Brazil's oldest and largest *favelas*, many clinging precariously to the city's steep slopes.

URBAN DEPRIVATION

Brazil's urban growth has created many problems. One of the major ones is to match people with jobs. Many migrants, once they move to the city, find it virtually impossible to find a job, and few other hopes are met. Their home turns out to be at best an inner-city slum, at worst a squatter's shack.

THE *FAVELAS*

Unable to find jobs and afford rented accommodation, Brazil's urban poor have built shantytowns on land to which they have no legal right. In Rio this usually means the hillsides that surround the city. The shantytowns take the name *favelas* from the flower that grows wild on these slopes, but there is nothing floral about the *favelas*. It is said that the only advantage enjoyed by the *favelados*, or slum dwellers, is the best views over Guanabara Bay. Seen from the shore, the *favelas* form a bizarre backdrop to the tourist resorts of Copacabana and Ipanema.

Rio is not the only city with *favelas*, but it has nearly 500, some of the oldest and the largest of them with populations estimated as high as 200,000. Most of the homes are little more than shacks built from any available material – wood, corrugated iron, plastic sheets, cardboard and reeds. Inside are one or two rooms with no running water, sanitation or electricity, unless it is illegally tapped. Typhoid, dysentery and other diseases are common in these overcrowded environments, where garbage rots in unpaved alleys.

The *favelados* are engaged in a daily struggle for survival made more difficult by a hazardous physical environment. Heavy rains on these steep slopes, weakened by construction work and the sheer weight of people, mean that flimsy structures can be carried downslope. There are frequent heavy death tolls as a result of these landslides.

There have been attempts to improve the living conditions in the *favelas*. Parts of Rocinho, a *favela* in Rio, have been supplied with electricity and running water, but no

The densely populated *favelas* are breeding grounds for disease, crime and violence.

sewerage system. Most of the improvements have come from self-help projects, which cannot provide more than a few services. Rocinho organizes walking tours for visitors, but most *favelas* are dangerous no-go areas, riddled with crime and ruled by drug traffickers and death squads. Many have long been abandoned by the authorities. In others, special police forces maintain some law and order.

CASE STUDY
STREET CHILDREN

Foraging for something to eat or sell is a daily chore for Brazil's street children.

As many as 12 million children in Brazil are forced to work instead of going to school. While most belong to *favela* families and return at night, others have no homes to go to. They sleep in doorways, under highway ramps, and even in sewers. These are the *abandonados*, or "deserted ones," Brazil's most tragic example of economic and social injustice.

Street children scrape a living doing whatever they can – selling goods, shining shoes, washing cars, stealing, or sifting through garbage. They are regularly exploited by adults, who use them as professional thieves, drug-runners or prostitutes. Brazil is estimated to have over half a million child prostitutes. There are reports of regular beatings by the authorities and, worst of all, murders carried out by paid vigilante groups. Charitable organizations such as UNICEF, the Red Cross and many religious groups do their best to help the situation, but without parents, schools, food or jobs, most street children have no choice but crime.

NEW CITIES: BRASÍLIA AND BELO HORIZONTE

The Brazilian government has long been concerned with the problems caused by the country's unequal distribution and density of population. Vast areas of empty land are regarded as national security risks, and the over-concentration of people and wealth in regions like the Southeast is considered damaging to the country as a whole. In 1960, the national capital was moved from Rio de Janeiro to Brasília, 970km to the northwest, in an attempt to rebalance the population spread. The aim was to create a major growth pole in Brazil's sparsely populated heartland, but the new capital was also seen as an important status symbol, one of the most grandiose and expensive projects Brazil has undertaken.

LOCATING THE CAPITAL

The idea of a capital situated away from the coast was first suggested in 1789. A century later, in 1891, the concept was written into the new Republic's constitution, but it was not until 1952 that the scheme actually happened, following extensive air and other surveys to find a suitable site. The one chosen was a 581km^2 location in the state of Goias, a sparsely inhabited piece of *cerrado* land directly on the watershed between the Amazon and Paraná Rivers. Construction began in 1957 and the main government and administrative buildings were

completed in three years. Brasília was a new metropolis, a city without a history, and this was reflected in its futuristic plan and architecture, the work of Lucio Costa and Oscar Niemeyer. What distinguishes Brasília from cities that have developed organically is the strict division between its functional zones: administration, business, housing, hotels and culture.

PLANS AND ARCHITECTURE

No one is certain whether the plan of Brasília was meant to resemble a cross, a bird or an airplane. Viewed from above it could be any of these (see city plan page 49). Since one of the first facilities to be completed was the airport (fast communications being essential), an airplane shape would have been a suitable choice. On its completion, the city's modern architecture caused a sensation, receiving both acclaim and criticism. UNESCO

Buildings like these apartment blocks have earned Brasília the description of "an elegant monotonous city."

includes it as one of its world cultural heritage sites but others have been less enthusiastic, seeing it as "elegant monotony" or "the moon's backside."

SUCCESS OR FAILURE?

Brasília's success is difficult to measure. Officially planned for a population of 1 million by 2000, Brasília reached this figure by 1986, 14 years early. The new capital did help to shift the country's political and economic center of gravity toward the northwest, as intended. However, there is much poverty in the city and the central area is ringed with large *favelas*, many of which started out as the temporary settlements of the construction workers. A comment by the planners puts Brasília into perspective: "It was not designed to solve Brazil's problems. It was bound to reflect them."

BELO HORIZONTE

Brasília was not the first modern Brazilian city to spring from a planner's drawing board. Belo Horizonte replaced the old colonial town of Ouro Preto in 1897 as the new state capital of Minas Gerais. Specially designed for its role, the city was laid out on a regular grid plan modeled on Washington, D.C. Today it is Brazil's third-largest city, a politically and culturally important center. However its wide, landscaped avenues and planned suburbs have suffered a high rate of urbanization over the last 60 years, and there are a large number of *favelas*. The city's name, meaning "Beautiful Horizon," seems misplaced today considering the horizon is usually obscured by air pollution from its steel, car manufacturing and textile industries.

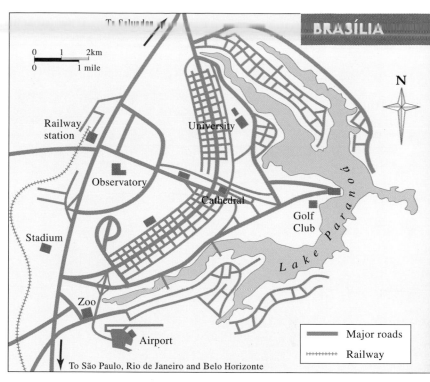

The "Crown of Thorns" cathedral is one of Brasília's daringly different public buildings.

TOURISM AND LEISURE

Recife's palm-fringed beaches and tropical climate help the Northeast's tourist industry.

Until recently, Brazil's tourist industry was poorly organized. Inadequate visitor facilities, high poverty levels and political troubles put off potential tourists. Another problem was the sheer distance of Brazil from the tourist supply region of the Northern Hemisphere, especially Western Europe. The neighboring countries of Argentina and Uruguay have been Brazil's main source of tourists, with increasing numbers arriving from the United States. Most European tourists are Portuguese, Italian and German, reflecting the country's immigration history.

CASE STUDY
RIO CARNIVAL

For many people, the thought of a holiday in Brazil conjures up images of cosmopolitan Rio de Janeiro and its famous carnival. Originally a purely religious festival held the week before Lent each year, this six-day party of music, dancing and costumed parades is celebrated throughout the country. But it is the Rio Carnival that is the most extravagant and world famous. Visitors from abroad and all over Brazil flock to the city every February, choking the airport, filling the hotels and inflating local prices. They are eager to be part of the world's largest and most colorful street festival.

Since the late 1970s EMBRATUR, the federal tourism agency, has been encouraging tourism throughout the country. It recognizes tourism as an important source of foreign currency and a way of improving Brazil's trade balance. As well as sponsoring city tourism, EMBRATUR gives financial support to beach resort development and to ecotourism in regions such as Amazonia.

RIO DE JANEIRO

Rio is Brazil's main entry point and tourism capital, with strong visitor attractions. The physical setting alone – with its mountain peaks, Copacabana and Ipanema beaches, and tropical rain forest within the city limits – more than justifies the title *Cidade Maravilhosa* ("Marvellous City"). Other attractions are the

Ecotourism in the Pantanal, where the activities of tourists are strictly controlled to prevent damage to the environment.

annual carnival, sophisticated shopping districts, museums and monuments, and a lively nightlife.

BEACH RESORTS

The Northeast states see tourism as a way of developing their economies and of slowing down their population out-migration. Modern airports such as those at Fortaleza, Recife and Salvador have links with many international cities, and a recent trend has been the growth in charter flights and package vacations. Tourists are attracted by the region's extensive beaches. The state of Ceará alone has over 500km of coastline, much of it unspoiled, but other areas are rapidly developing as busy international resorts. This development can be seen in the area around Jericoacoara, once a down-market hippy center whose beach is regarded as one of the world's most beautiful. It is still popular with backpackers but has recently attracted package tour groups staying in purpose-built hotels.

AMAZONIAN TOURISM

Uncontrolled tourism would be another threat to the Amazon rain forest. So far, visitor numbers have been limited and the many tourist agencies support ecotourism and forest sustainability. The famous Amazon Village is an eco-lodge on the shores of Lake Puraquequara, 30km from Manaus. Accommodation is in simple wooden bungalows and there is no electricity. Visitors can take trips into the rain forest and come into direct contact with its plants, animals and Amerindians.

HERITAGE TOURISM

Brazil has a rich heritage of colonial monuments ranging from forts, country houses and churches to entire old towns, which are now under protection. UNESCO has helped to promote their tourist appeal by making some of them world cultural heritage centers.

The historic core of Salvador is an example. From 1500 to 1815 Salvador was Brazil's busiest port, growing rich on sugar, gold and diamonds. Its wealth can be seen in the city's magnificent merchant houses and elaborate, gold-decorated churches. Olinda, a few kilometers north of Recife, is another protected town with sixteenth- and seventeenth-century churches and palaces. But it is Ouro Preto, the old state capital of Minas Gerais, that has Brazil's finest assembly of colonial architecture. The town has many Baroque churches set in an authentic townscape of unplanned, narrow and winding streets. The churches contain religious works of art by Brazil's famous architect and sculptor, Antonio Francisco Lisboa (1738–1814).

Tourism in the Amazon supports small-scale handicraft projects like this one, where money paid for the handicrafts goes straight to the people who made them.

The high-tech equipment used in this São Paulo hospital is in sharp contrast to the average standard of medical equipment in Brazil.

QUALITY OF LIFE AND LEISURE

People's quality of life (their housing, diet, healthcare and income, for example) varies throughout Brazil. There are major differences in both rural and urban areas. The country's per-capita GNP is low compared with developed countries, and there are vast inequalities in the distribution of wealth. The poorest 20 percent of Brazil's population share only 2.5 percent of the country's wealth. In comparison, the richest 20 percent share between themselves 63.7 percent of the total wealth.

A "BELINDA" COUNTRY

Over 60 million Brazilians live in poverty. Many millions live without clean tap water, sewerage systems or proper health services.

Over 15 percent of the country's youngest children suffer from malnutrition. In some areas, infant mortality is 40 times higher than the average for Europe. A third of the population is illiterate. For these and other reasons, Brazil has been described as "Belinda," a country with an economic potential similar to Belgium but with social problems similar to parts of India. In Brazil, a small affluent First-World society lives alongside those trapped in a Third-World cycle of poverty.

EDUCATION AND HEALTH

The low priority given to education is a key factor explaining Brazil's poverty. Many rural and urban children have never attended school, or leave at the earliest opportunity without qualifications. It is estimated that some 40 percent of Brazilians over 15 are not capable of reading and understanding a newspaper. This means that there are few possibilities of their finding work except in menial and poorly paid jobs. The uneducated are trapped in a disadvantaged lifestyle.

Poor health services do not help. Those who can afford it have access to advanced medical facilities, but for the rest of the population there is a chronic shortage of medical

Brazil needs to spend more money on schools to improve its literacy levels.

A carnival procession by a Candomblé religious group in Salvador. The Candomblé religion combines elements of West African and Christian faiths.

personnel, hospitals and medicines. Traveling bus and riverboat clinics provide medical help in remote areas, but the poor get little treatment for diseases such as cholera, pesticide poisoning or, increasingly, AIDS.

LEISURE TIME

As in all countries there is a firm link in Brazil between leisure activities and available wealth. Some of the biggest differences are seen in the major cities, where the wealthy enjoy an affluent life of restaurants, bars and night clubs that are beyond the reach of a large section of the population. There are, however, certain activities in which all Brazilians can take part, regardless of social class and financial status.

Soccer (known here as football) is Brazil's most popular leisure activity. The game is played everywhere – on beaches, in the streets and on any piece of vacant ground. It is watched by millions on television or in huge stadiums such as Rio's Maracaná, which has a crowd capacity of 150,000. Many young Brazilians dream of becoming soccer stars. In coastal cities such as Rio and Salvador, Brazil also has a well-developed beach culture. Beach activities include volleyball, which is another popular Brazilian sport.

RELIGION

Many Brazilian festivals and holidays are related to religion. Although Brazil claims to have the largest Catholic population of any country in the world, there are a great variety of other religions. Some religions, such as Candomblé, Umbanda and Macumba, combine elements from a number of different faiths. The main influences are from Amerindian beliefs, Christianity and African religions brought to Brazil during the slave era. Many Brazilians practice their own individualized religion, including Christian saints, Indian idols and African deities in their worship and prayers.

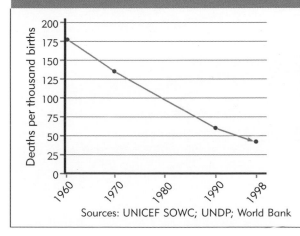

UNDER-FIVE MORTALITY RATE

Deaths per thousand births

Sources: UNICEF SOWC; UNDP; World Bank

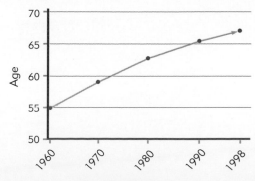

LIFE EXPECTANCY AT BIRTH

Age

Source: WHO (World Health Organization)

The dam at the Itaipú hydroelectric power station cost over US$25 billion.

Despite its huge size and population, Brazil has not played a major political role in shaping the world. Economically, however, especially with products such as rubber, sugar, coffee and minerals, it has long been linked to the world economy. Today the processes of globalization affect almost every aspect of the country's economic and social life. Much is related to the fact that Brazil owes vast sums of money to foreign banks and financial institutions.

NATIONAL DEBT

Between 1964 and 1985, when the military governed the country, Brazil borrowed huge amounts of money from abroad. The money was used to build roads, hydroelectric power stations, and the new capital of Brasília, and to search for minerals. The borrowing helped the country's economic progress, but much was wasted on poorly planned, large-scale projects instead of being spent on education, housing and medical services. In 1999, the Brazilian national debt was quoted as US$232 billion. This is the equivalent of US$1,399 for every Brazilian man, woman and child.

Many argue that Brazil's national debt has increased the country's social and economic

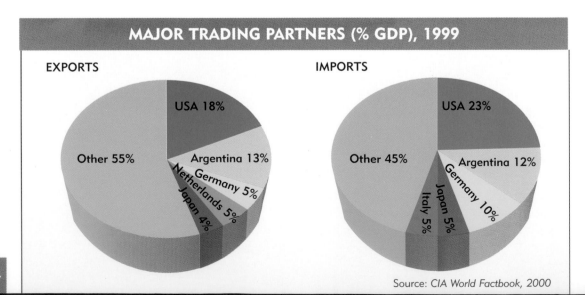

MAJOR TRADING PARTNERS (% GDP), 1999

EXPORTS

- USA 18%
- Argentina 13%
- Germany 5%
- Netherlands 5%
- Japan 4%
- Other 55%

IMPORTS

- USA 23%
- Argentina 12%
- Germany 10%
- Japan 5%
- Italy 5%
- Other 45%

Source: CIA World Factbook, 2000

inequalities. Repayment to foreign banks absorbs about 70 percent of earnings from Brazilian exports, and constantly rising interest rates have increased this burden. As an alternative method of repayment, banks have agreed to receive company and other investment shares in Brazilian businesses. This has led to further global involvement in the country's economy.

TRADING PARTNERS

Brazil's main trading links are with (in descending order) the EU, North America, Asia and the Middle East. As the wealthiest country in South America, it has a big influence on improving the whole continent's economy. An important part of South American trade is through MERCOSUL, a union currently linking Brazil, Argentina, Paraguay and Uruguay, which lets each country trade with the others free of tax. This makes the imported products cheaper than imports from Western countries, so it helps countries in the union. Other South American countries are interested in joining this common market, whose goal is to create a trade area that is less dependant on Western countries.

SPORTING WORLD

Brazil is often in the world's headlines for its sporting achievements. Mention Brazil and many people will think of soccer. Even those little interested in the game will have heard of

Products from small-scale organic farms, like this organic pepper farm in Bahia, fetch higher prices in Brazil than products sold to the international market.

Brazilian players, not least Pelé (Edson Arantes do Nascimento), internationally acclaimed as one of the world's greatest soccer players. The Brazilian team has been the first to win the World Cup four times, in 1958, 1962, 1970 and 1994. To win is a great source of national pride; to lose is a national disaster.

Another of Brazil's major contributions to the sporting world is its success in auto racing, with names such as Emerson Fittipaldi, Nelson Piquet and Ayrton Senna. Since the 1970s, Brazil has won more Formula One Grand Prix championships than any other country.

MUSIC

It is said that the Brazilians are among the most musical people in the world. The country's popular music, shaped by the rhythms of three continents, has achieved international success. The samba (hallmark of the Rio carnival), bossa nova, lambada and other musical styles have taken the sounds and atmosphere of Brazil to all parts of the world.

Hundreds gather to watch the soccer World Cup on a huge outdoor screen.

Only a small proportion of Brazilians can shop in stores like these. The struggle to close the gap between rich and poor is one of Brazil's biggest challenges.

LAND OF THE FUTURE

Some people say that Brazil is the "land of the future." From the arrival of the first Europeans in the early sixteenth century, Brazil's vast South American territory has been a land of great opportunity. Land, forests, water and minerals provided great potential for many rich lifestyles. Yet compared with modern industrialized countries, Brazil is still a poor nation, and there is a huge gap between the rich and the poor.

In the countryside and the cities, Brazil's wealthy live in large, closely guarded mansions and villas. They move around in chauffeur-driven cars and often have armed bodyguards to protect them from kidnappers. In contrast are the country's urban slums, overcrowded with undernourished youngsters. This gap between rich and poor is because Brazil has always been dominated, both economically and politically, by a small, influential elite. Despite important changes of government, this minority still controls the country. The elite own huge areas of land, and because land equals wealth in Brazil, this is a major cause of social inequality. Until there are major land reforms and redistribution, Brazil's social inequality will continue.

CONSERVATION AND THE ENVIRONMENT

In its natural state, the Amazon rain forest is an almost perfectly closed ecosystem, but it can easily be disrupted by outside pressures. Many authorities consider the results of rain-forest interference to be the world's most serious land-use problem. But Amazonia is not the only region of threatened habitats. Brazil's Atlantic forest, home of the tamarin monkeys and other endangered species, has been reduced to some 7 percent of its original cover. The rest has been taken over by cattle pastures, cultivation and urbanization. As with other parts of Brazil, scientists are calling for an increase in eco-agriculture, a way of increasing food production through new land use policies rather than encroaching into natural areas.

In June 1992, an international conference about the environment was held in Rio, called the Rio Summit. Reports from the conference stressed the importance of Brazil

PERSONAL COMPUTERS

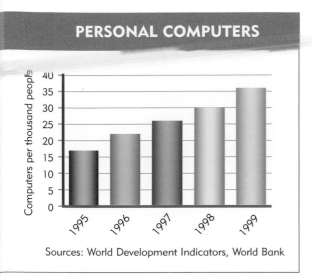

Computers per thousand people

	1995	1996	1997	1998	1999

Sources: World Development Indicators, World Bank

RIGHT: Without basic education or skills, people earn money in any way they can.

to the protection of the world environment. The conference made it clear that many countries are responsible for what is happening in Amazonia, where interference with the region's ecosystems has led to the "greenhouse effect" and "global warming." The same issues were raised at the 1997 Convention on Climate Change in Kyoto, Japan. It was made clear that protection of Brazil's environment must be the responsibility of the world, as well as Brazil, if the world climate is to be protected in the future.

The uakari monkey is just one of many species threatened by development in the Amazon.

BRAZIL'S PEOPLE – A VALUABLE RESOURCE

With about 70 percent of its population under age 30, Brazil is a young nation full of new ideas, dreams and boundless energy. Together with its natural resources, a growing financial sector and a core of educated business managers, Brazil's people give it the potential to become a major world power.

GLOSSARY

Agrarian Having to do with land and its farming use.

Agribusinesses Businesses associated with farming.

Baroque A style of art and architecture that flourished between the sixteenth and eighteenth centuries.

Black market The exchange of illegally acquired and traded goods.

Cash crop A crop grown for sale rather than local use.

Consumer goods Manufactured goods to be sold directly to people, such as clothes and food.

Conurbations Large urban areas created by the linking together of several towns.

Dictatorship A form of government in which an individual, a committee, or a group holds absolute power.

Drainage basin The area that is drained by a river and its tributaries.

Ecologists People who are specialists in ecology, the study of the relationship of plants and animals to their environment.

Ecosystem A community of plants and animals, and the environment in which they live.

Ecotourism A type of tourism that tries to protect the environment.

Elite A small number of rich and powerful people or organizations.

Favelas Shantytowns, or slums.

Favelados The Brazilian name for people who live in the *favelas*, or shantytowns.

Federal government A system of government in which political power is divided between a central government and smaller units, such as states.

GDP Gross domestic product is the volume of goods and services produced annually in a country, but excluding earnings from overseas.

Global warming The gradual warming of the surface of the planet as a result of a change in the composition of atmospheric gases, especially an increase in the percentage of carbon dioxide.

GMT Greenwich Mean Time, the time at Greenwich, England, which was made the starting point of the world's time zones in 1884.

GNP Gross National Product is the volume of goods and services produced annually within a country, which includes earnings from overseas.

Greenhouse gases Gases that help to trap warmth in the atmosphere, which contributes to global warming.

Growth pole A region where the growth of industries and development has caused other growth in a chain reaction.

Hydroelectric power stations Structures designed to generate electricity by using the power of water.

Inflation A general increase in prices.

Intensive farming A type of farming that requires a high level of labor and money.

Microclimate The local climate of a very small part of the world.

Migrant A person who moves away from his or her home. The move can be temporary, like a period of working abroad, or permanent.

Monoculture Concentrating on a single product on a farm.

Multinationals Large companies that have factories or offices in more than one country.

Pampas The name given to the mostly treeless plains of South America south of the Amazon.

Primary forest The original forest cover of an area.

Privatization Ownership by individuals rather than the government.

Quality of life The level of economic, social and environmental satisfaction experienced by a person or community.

Scrubland An area of dry poor soil supporting stunted trees and shrubs, as in the Brazilian *sertão*.

Secondary forest Forest that grows once the original trees have been cut down.

Trade balance A country's profit or loss from the value of its imports and exports.

Tropical climate A climate of constant high temperatures and rainfall found between the Tropics of Capricorn and Cancer.

UNESCO United Nations Educational, Scientific and Cultural Organization, a part of the UN that promotes education, communication and the arts.

Urbanization The growth of urban areas.

Watershed The area separating streams that flow into different drainage basins.

FURTHER INFORMATION

BOOKS TO READ:

Chinery, Michael. *Secrets of the Rainforest* [illegible] Lt. Guelmmuuu, Ontario: Crabtree, 1999–2000. Titles on people, plants, animals and conservation issues in tropical rain forests.

Cleary, David et al. *The Rough Guide to Brazil.* London: Rough Guides, Ltd., 2000. A comprehensive handbook to Brazil, with practical tips and region-by-region commentary.

de Carvalho, Sarah. *The Street Children of Brazil.* London: Hodder & Stoughton Religious, 1996. Follows an Englishwoman's experience of working for a missionary organization in Brazil helping street children.

Hecht, Tobias. *At Home in the Street: Street Children of Northeast Brazil.* Cambridge: Cambridge University Press, 1998. Based on fieldwork among the children themselves, this book examines the lives of Brazilian street children.

Lewington, Anna and Edward Parker. *Antonio's Rainforest.* Minneapolis, Minnesota: Carolrhoda Books, 1993. Looks at the life of a rubber tapper's son in the Amazon.

Lewington, Anna. *Atlas of the Rain Forests.* Milwaukee, Wisconsin: Raintree Publishers, 1997. Looks at peoples, plants and animals in rain forests around the world.

Morrison, Marion. *Country Fact Files: Brazil.* Milwaukee, Wisconsin: Raintree Publishers, 1994. Illustrated reference for ages 9 to 13.

Parker, Edward. *The Changing Face of Brazil.* Milwaukee, Wisconsin: Raintree Publishers, 2002. Illustrated reference for ages 9 and up.

Robinson, Roger. *Country Studies: Brazil.* Crystal Lake, Illinois: Heinman Library, 1999.

Smart, Chris and Steve Lockwood. *Exploring Brazil.* London: Hodder & Stoughton Educational, 1994. In-depth study of Brazil for young readers.

WEBSITES:

GENERAL INFORMATION ON BRAZIL
Brazilinfo.com
http://www.brazilinfo.com
Click on the British flag for the English version of this site, which provides general information on Brazil including features on its national parks, history and general statistics.

Brazilian Embassy
http://www.brasilemb.org/

GENERAL STATISTICS
Brazil: The World Factbook
http://www.cia.gov/cia/publications/factbook/geos/br.html

SÃO PAULO
São Paulo State Government
http://www.saopaulo.sp.gov.br/home/index.htm
Click on the English version icon for information on tourism, culture and the history of São Paulo.

RIO DE JANEIRO
Rio State Government
http://www.governo.rj.gov.br
Click on the English version icon.

METRIC CONVERSION TABLE

To convert	to	do this
mm (millimeters)	inches	divide by 25.4
cm (centimeters)	inches	divide by 2.54
m (meters)	feet	multiply by 3.281
m (meters)	yards	multiply by 1.094
km (kilometers)	yards	multiply by 1094
km (kilometers)	miles	divide by 1.6093
kilometers per hour	miles per hour	divide by 1.6093
cm² (square centimeters)	square inches	divide by 6.452
m² (square meters)	square feet	multiply by 10.76
m² (square meters)	square yards	multiply by 1.196
km² (square kilometers)	square miles	divide by 2.59
km² (square kilometers)	acres	multiply by 247.1
hectares	acres	multiply by 2.471
cm³ (cubic centimeters)	cubic inches	multiply by 16.387
m³ (cubic meters)	cubic yards	multiply by 1.308
l (liters)	pints	multiply by 2.113
l (liters)	gallons	divide by 3.785
g (grams)	ounces	divide by 28.329
kg (kilograms)	pounds	multiply by 2.205
metric tonnes	short tons	multiply by 1.1023
metric tonnes	long tons	multiply by 0.9842
BTUs (British thermal units)	kWh (kilowatt-hours)	divide by 3,415.3
watts	horsepower	multiply by 0.001341
kWh (kilowatt-hours)	horsepower-hours	multiply by 1.341
MW (megawatts)	horsepower	multiply by 1,341
gigawatts per hour	horsepower per hour	multiply by 1,341,000
°C (degrees Celsius)	°F (degrees Fahrenheit)	multiply by 1.8 then add 32

INDEX

Numbers shown in **bold** refer to pages with maps, graphic illustrations or photographs.

Jaguars live in the rain forests of Brazil, but they are becoming increasingly rare.

Rio de Janeiro's most famous landmark – the statue of Christ the Redeemer – shrouded in mist.